THE PHILLIP KEVEREN SERIES EASY PIANO

TV THEMES

> — PIANO LEVEL —
> **EARLY INTERMEDIATE/INTERMEDIATE**
> (HLSPL LEVEL 4-5)

ISBN 978-0-634-06981-9

HAL•LEONARD®
CORPORATION
7777 W. BLUEMOUND RD. P.O. BOX 13819 MILWAUKEE, WI 53213

Visit Hal Leonard Online at
www.halleonard.com

Visit Phillip at
www.phillipkeveren.com

PREFACE

Television themes are designed to create a positive musical impression in one minute or less. To that end, the tunes are catchy and often impossible to forget. Musical fads come and go, and TV themes reflect these evolving tastes. They become snapshots of the era in which they first jumped out of the tube and into our lives.

What I find particularly interesting about this music is its cross-generational appeal. Try playing "name that tune" at your next family gathering. It's hard to say whether grandparent or grandchild can identify "I Love Lucy" first! Thanks to re-run heaven, many of these tunes live on and on.

So, turn off the TV, sit down at the piano, and have a little fun!

With best wishes,
Phillip Keveren

BIOGRAPHY

Phillip Keveren, a multi-talented keyboard artist and composer, has composed original works in a variety of genres from piano solo to symphonic orchestra. Mr. Keveren gives frequent concerts and workshops for teachers and their students in the United States, Canada, Europe, and Asia. Mr. Keveren holds a B.M. in composition from California State University Northridge and a M.M. in composition from the University of Southern California.

CONTENTS

THE ADDAMS FAMILY THEME
Theme from the TV Show and Movie

Music and Lyrics by VIC MIZZY
Arranged by Phillip Keveren

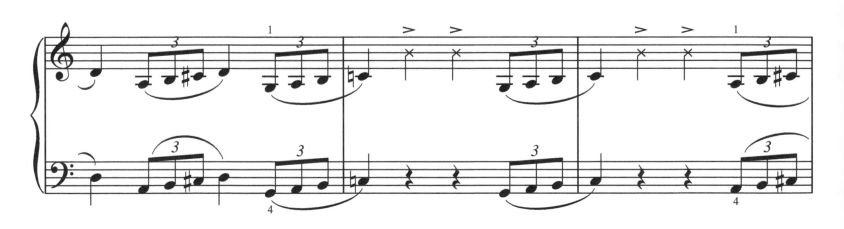

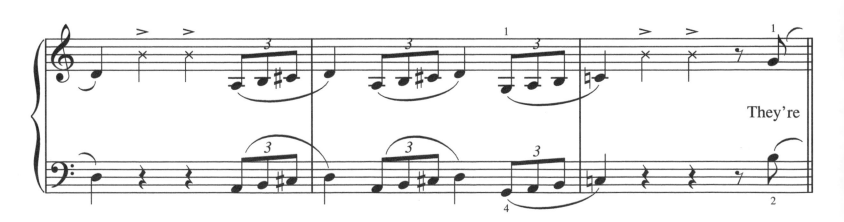

THEME FROM "BEWITCHED"

from the Television Series

Words and Music by JACK KELLER
and HOWARD GREENFIELD
Arranged by Phillip Keveren

THE BRADY BUNCH
Theme from the Paramount Television Series THE BRADY BUNCH

Words and Music by SHERWOOD SCHWARTZ
and FRANK DEVOL
Arranged by Phillip Keveren

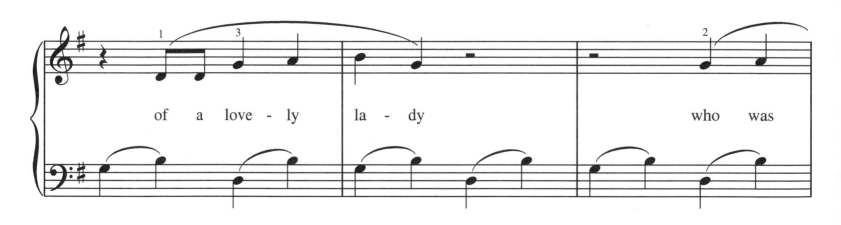

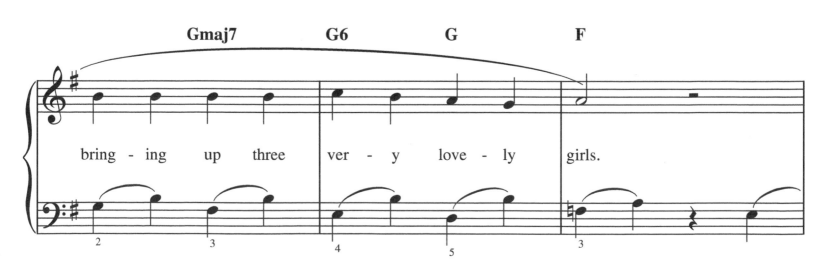

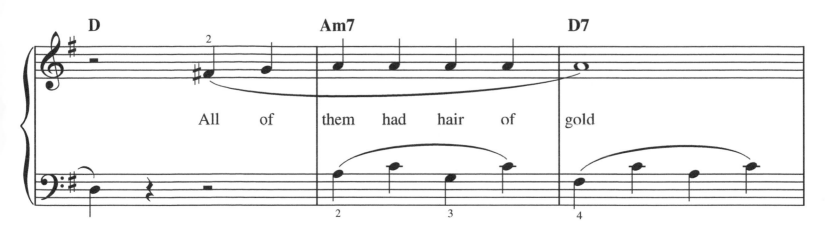

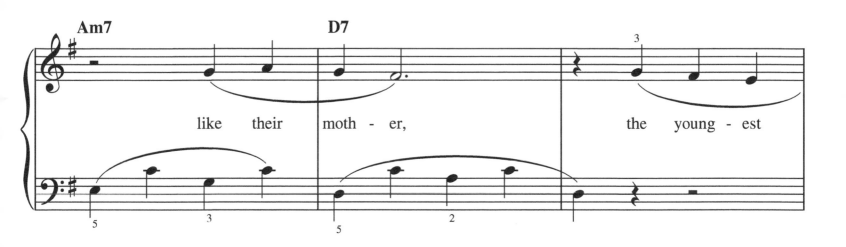

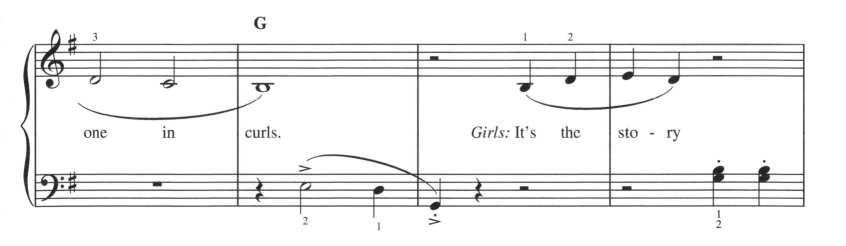

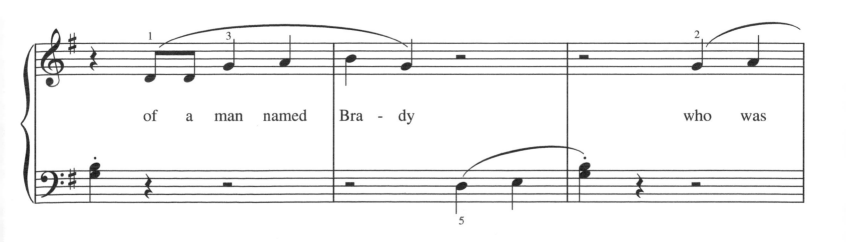

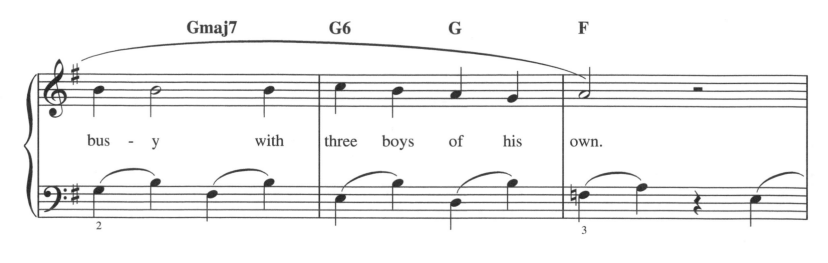

bus - y with three boys of his own.

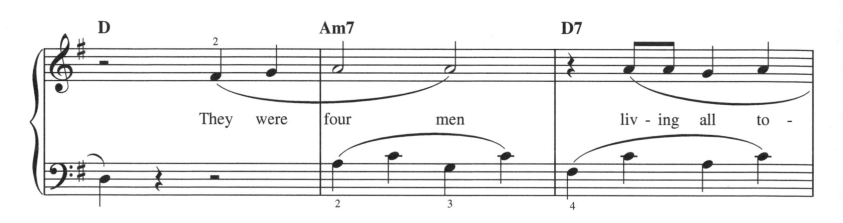

They were four men liv - ing all to -

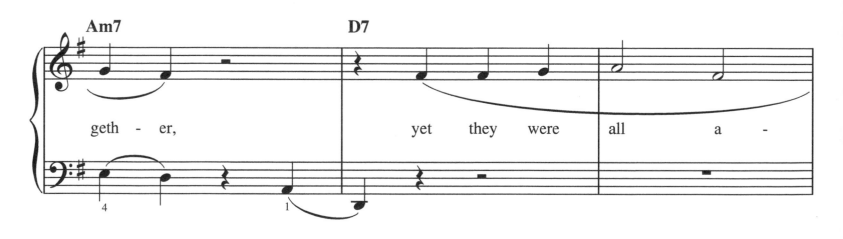

geth - er, yet they were all a -

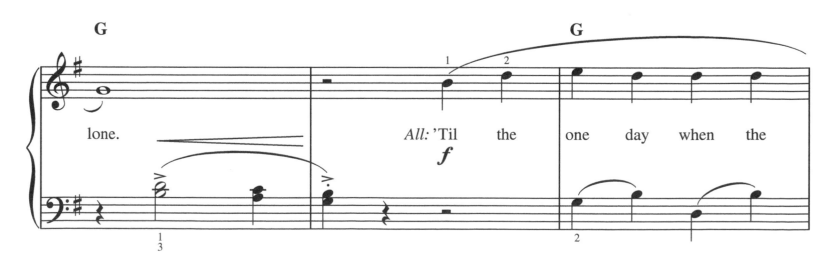

lone.

All: 'Til the one day when the

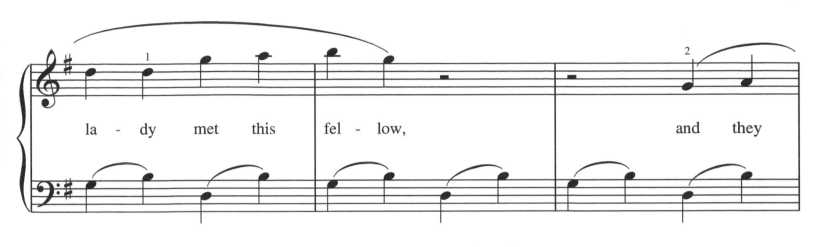

la - dy met this fel - low, and they

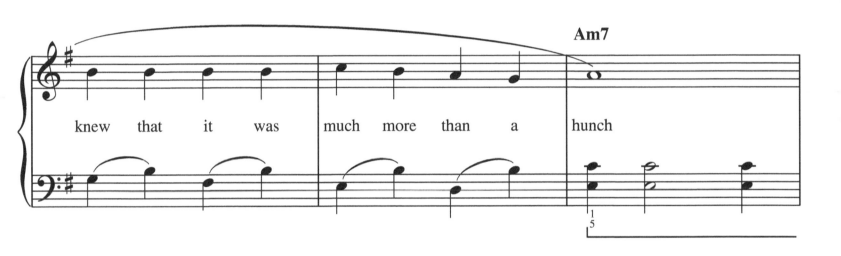

knew that it was much more than a hunch

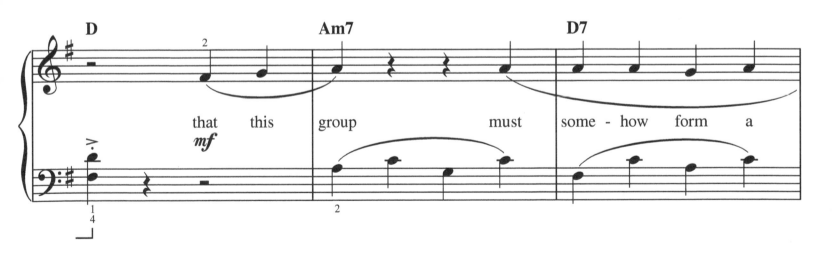

that this group must some - how form a

mf

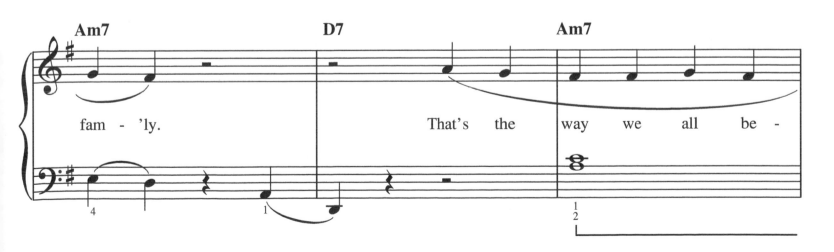

fam - 'ly. That's the way we all be -

I LOVE LUCY

from the Television Series

Lyric by HAROLD ADAMSON
Music by ELIOT DANIEL
Arranged by Phillip Keveren

Bright Show tempo

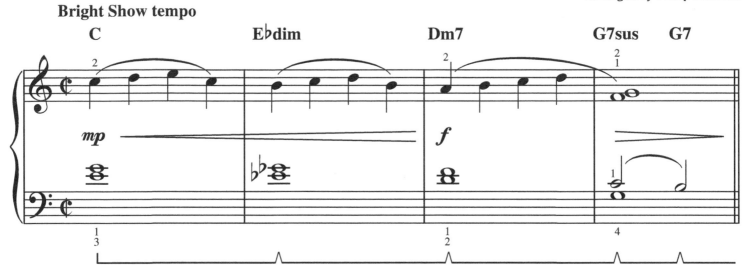

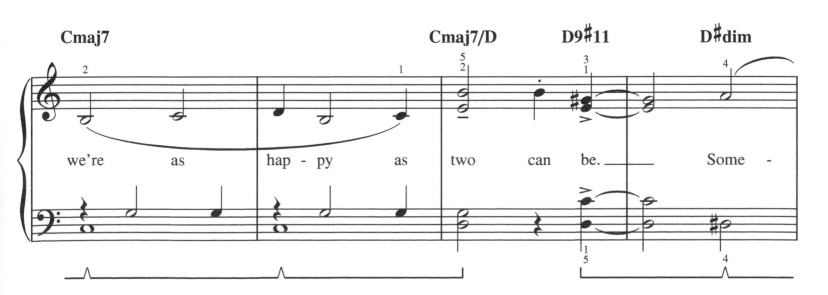

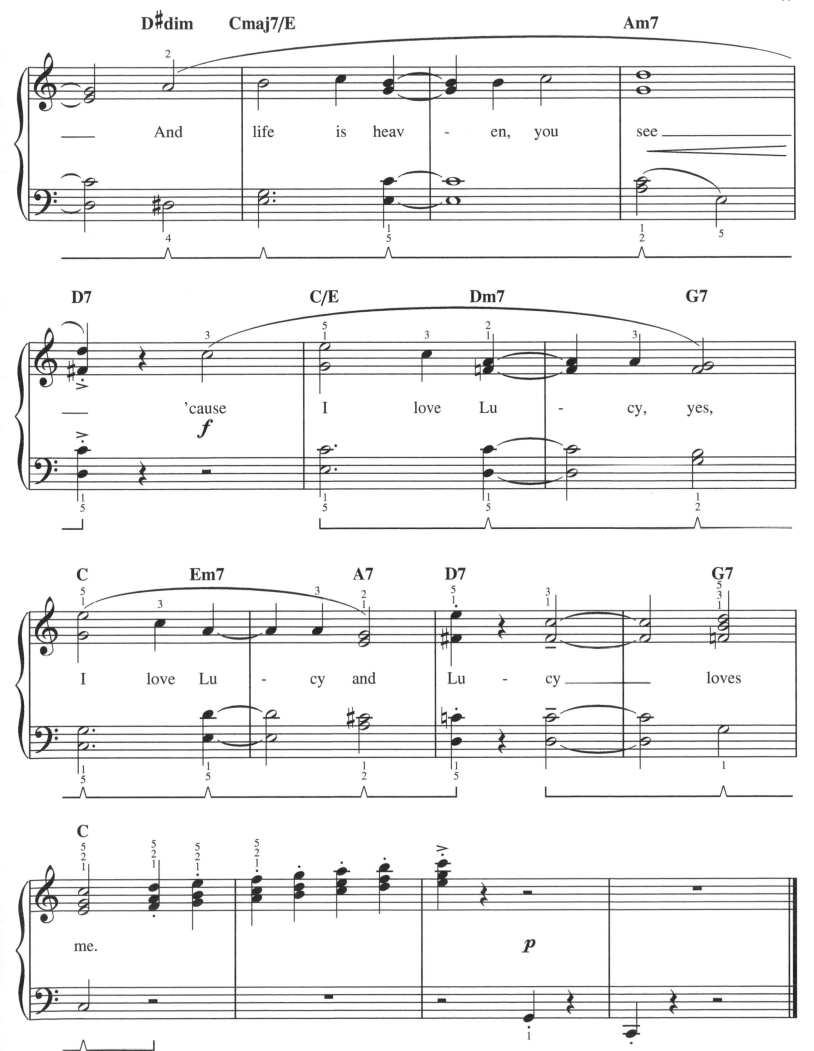

HAPPY DAYS
Theme from the Paramount Television Series HAPPY DAYS

Words by NORMAN GIMBEL
Music by CHARLES FOX
Arranged by Phillip Keveren

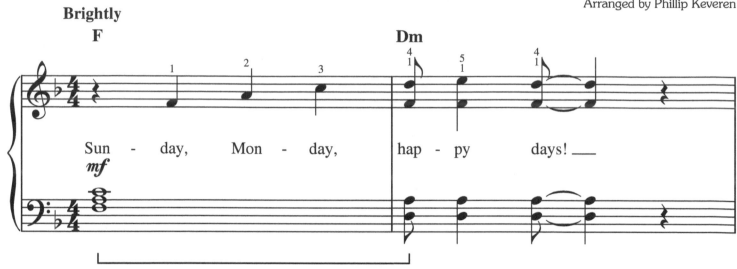

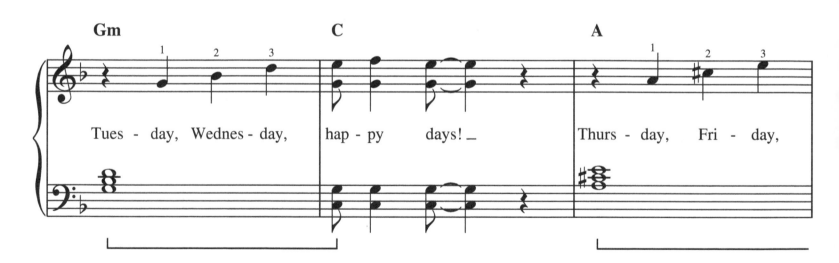

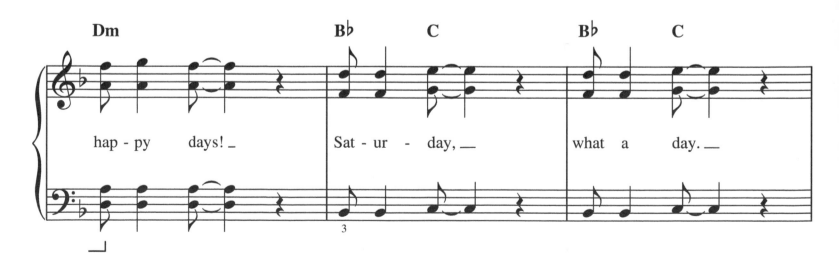

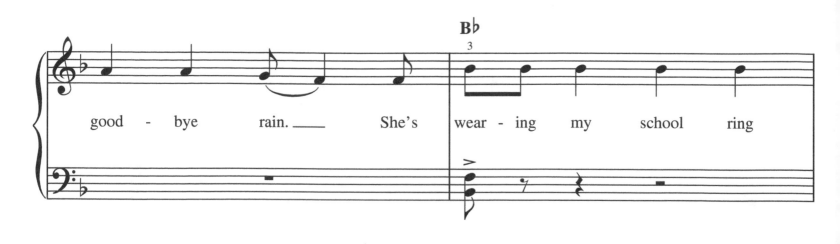

good - bye rain. ____ She's wear - ing my school ring

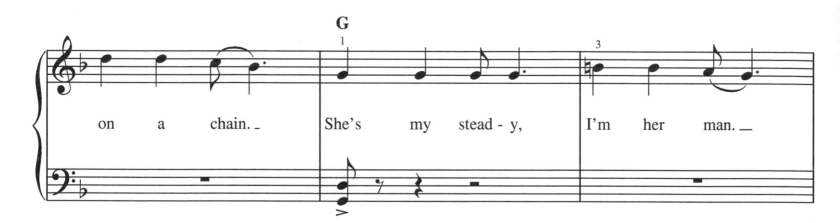

on a chain. _ She's my stead - y, I'm her man. _

I'm gon - na love her all I can. This day is ours. _

_____ (Won't you be mine?)

I'M SO GLAD WE HAD THIS TIME TOGETHER

Carol Burnett's Theme from THE CAROL BURNETT SHOW

By JOE HAMILTON
Arranged by Phillip Keveren

Slowly, reflectively

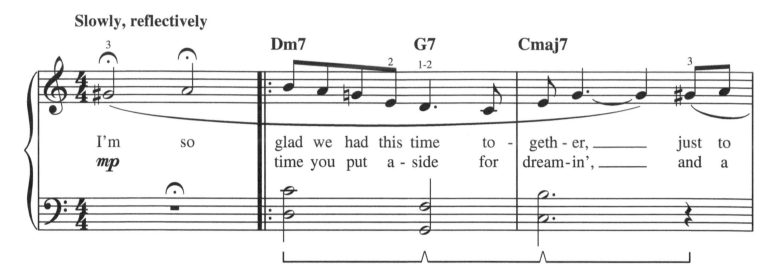

I'm   so   glad we had this time   to - geth - er, _____   just to
        time you put a - side for   dream-in', _____   and a

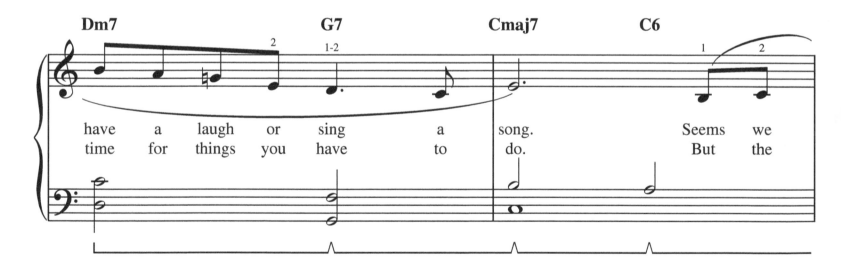

have   a   laugh   or   sing   a   song.   Seems   we
time   for   things   you   have   to   do.   But   the

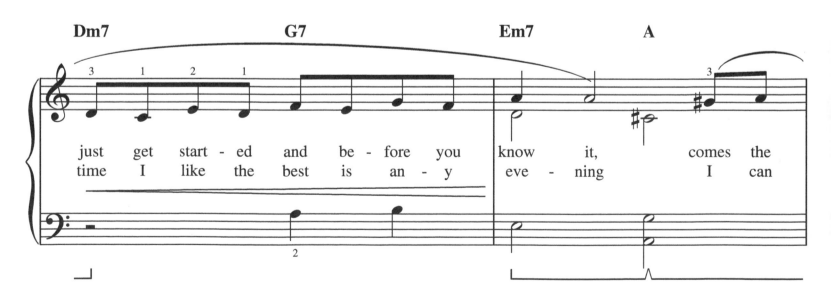

just   get   start - ed   and   be - fore   you   know   it,   comes   the
time   I   like   the   best   is   an - y   eve - ning   I   can

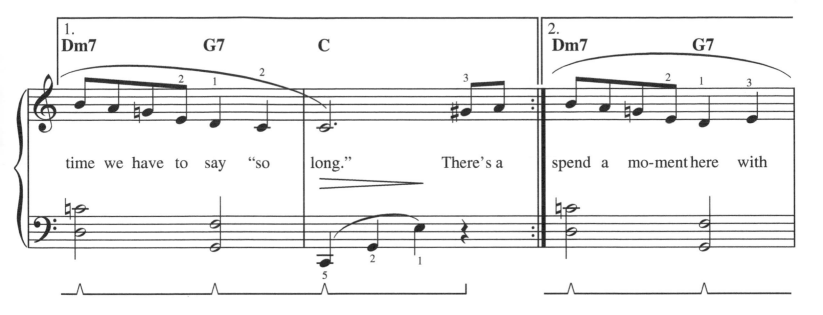

1. **Dm7**　　　**G7**　　　**C**

time we have to say "so long." There's a

2. **Dm7**　　　**G7**

spend a mo-ment here with

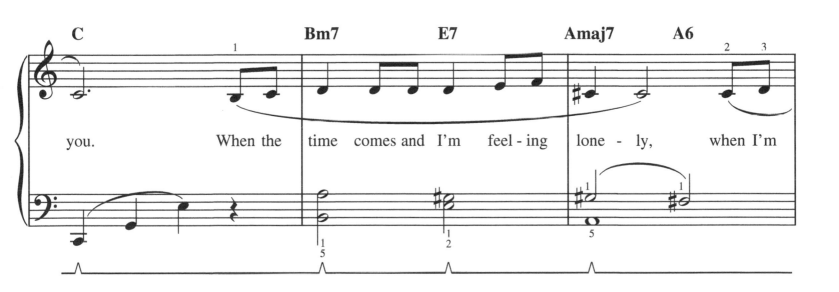

C　　　**Bm7**　　**E7**　　　**Amaj7**　　**A6**

you. When the time comes and I'm feel - ing lone - ly, when I'm

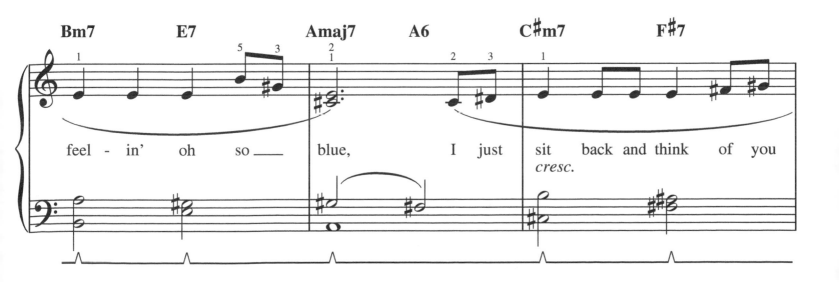

Bm7　　**E7**　　　**Amaj7**　　**A6**　　　**C♯m7**　　**F♯7**

feel - in' oh so ____ blue, I just sit back and think of you

cresc.

JEANNIE
Theme from I DREAM OF JEANNIE

By HUGH MONTENEGRO
and BUDDY KAYE
Arranged by Phillip Keveren

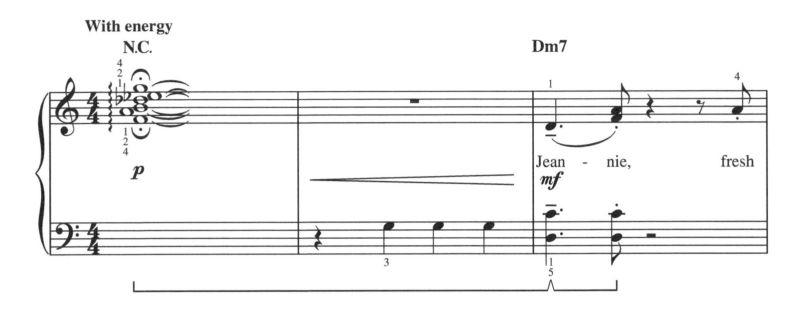

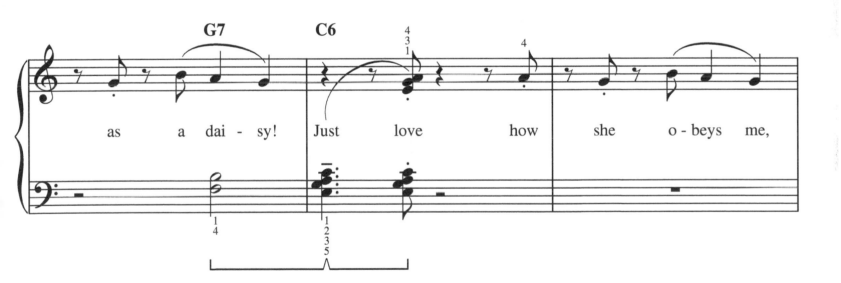

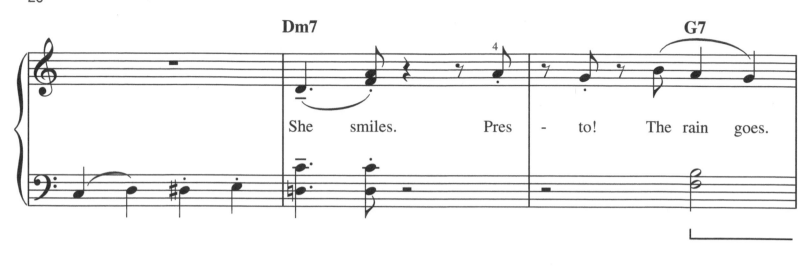

She smiles. Pres - to! The rain goes.

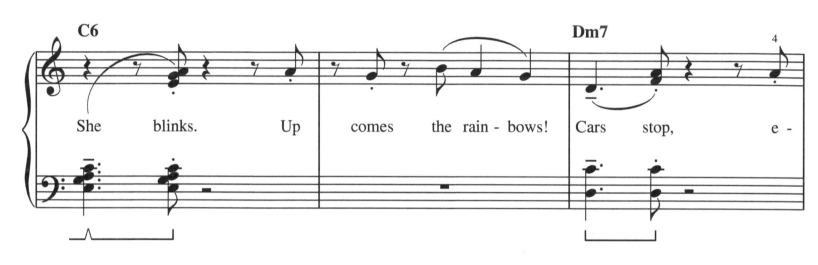

She blinks. Up comes the rain - bows! Cars stop, e -

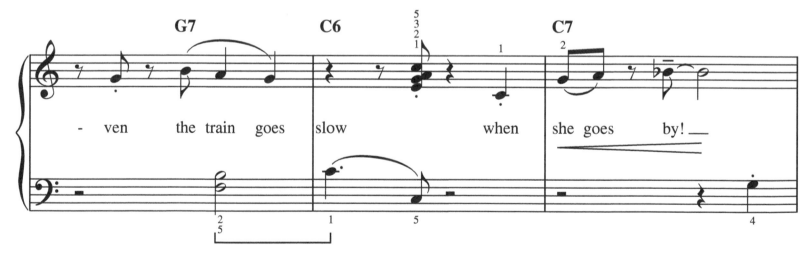

- ven the train goes slow when she goes by! ___

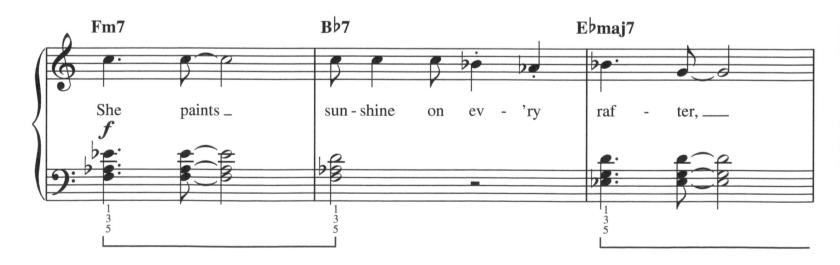

She paints ___ sun - shine on ev - 'ry raf - ter, ___

LINUS AND LUCY

By VINCE GUARALDI
Arranged by Phillip Keveren

Moderately fast (♩ = 152)

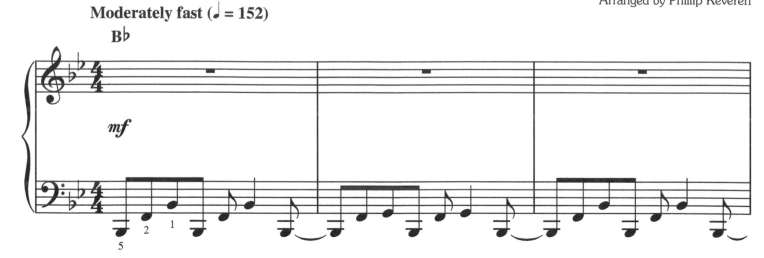

THE LITTLE HOUSE
(On the Prairie)
Theme from the TV Series

Music by DAVID ROSE
Arranged by Phillip Keveren

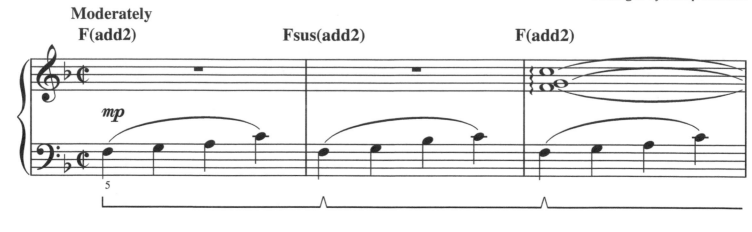

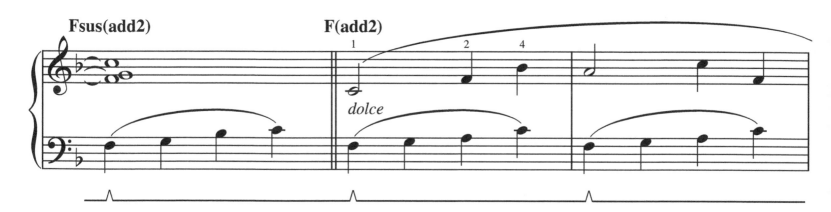

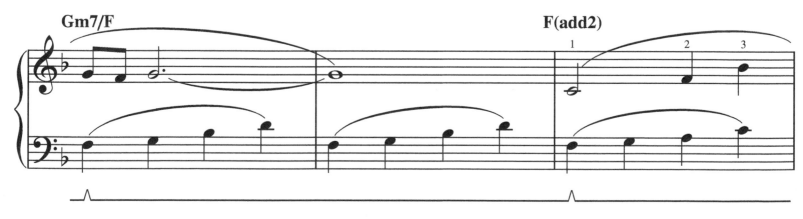

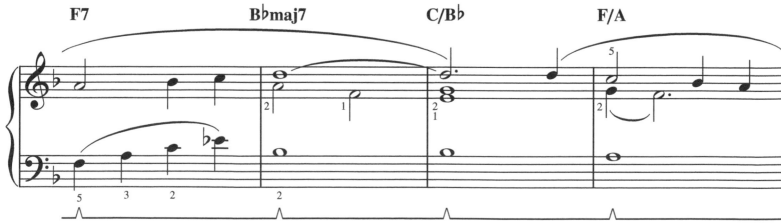

MISSION: IMPOSSIBLE THEME

from the Paramount Television Series MISSION: IMPOSSIBLE

By LALO SCHIFRIN
Arranged by Phillip Keveren

Moderately, with drive

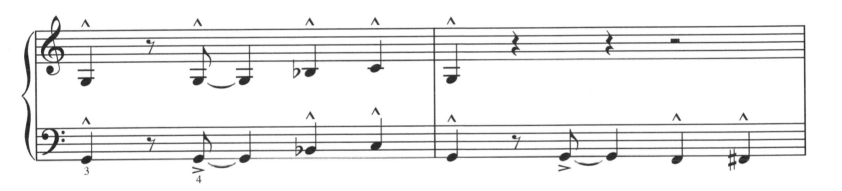

LOVE BOAT THEME
from the Television Series

Words and Music by CHARLES FOX
and PAUL WILLIAMS
Arranged by Phillip Keveren

Moderate Disco

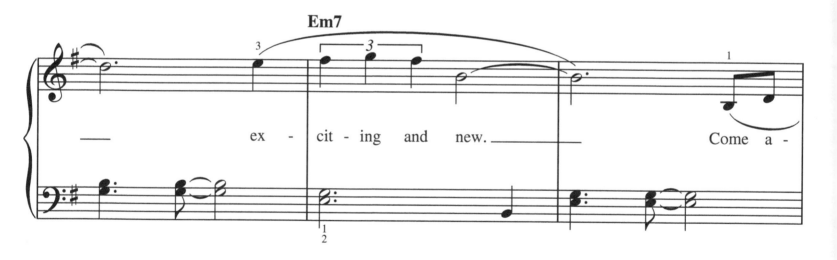

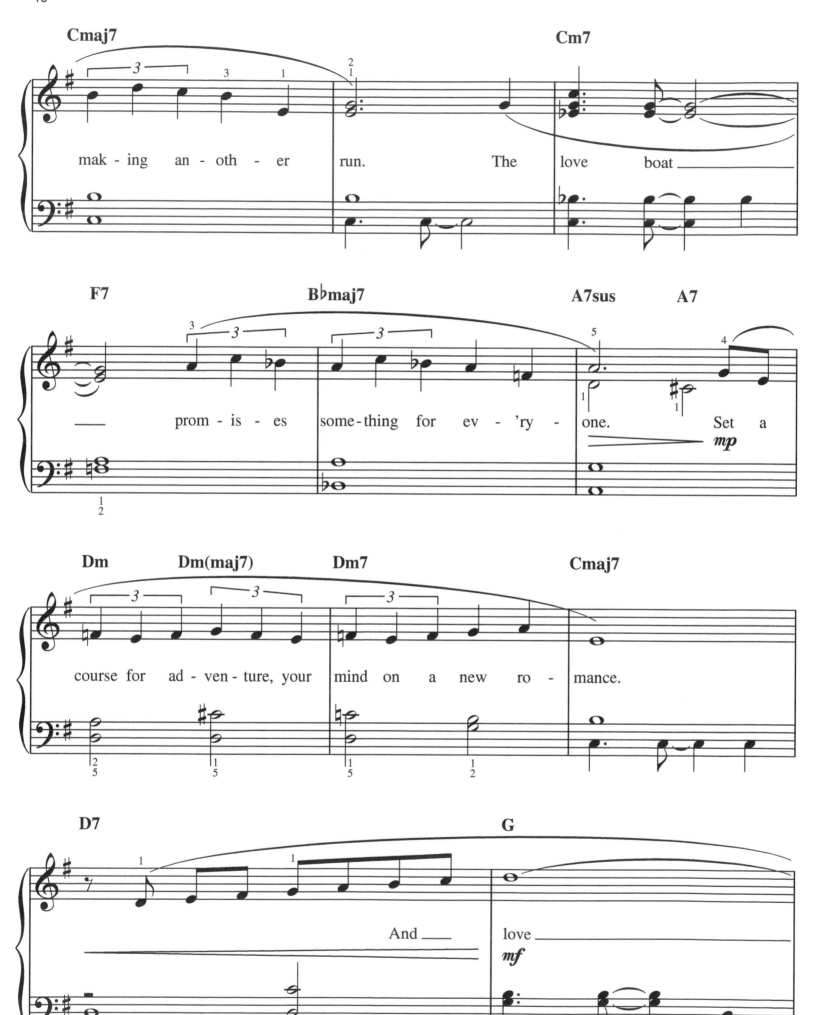

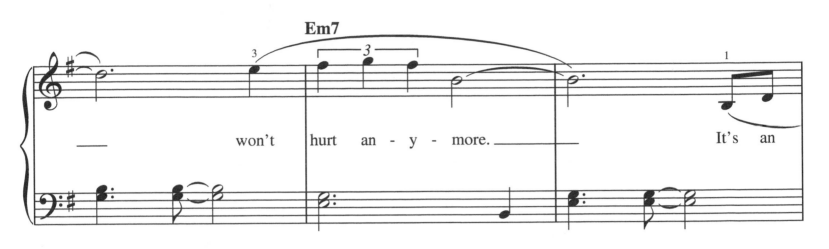

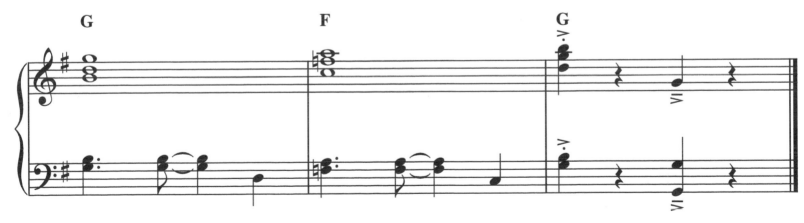

THE ODD COUPLE
Theme from the Paramount Television Series THE ODD COUPLE

Words by SAMMY CAHN
Music by NEAL HEFTI
Arranged by Phillip Keveren

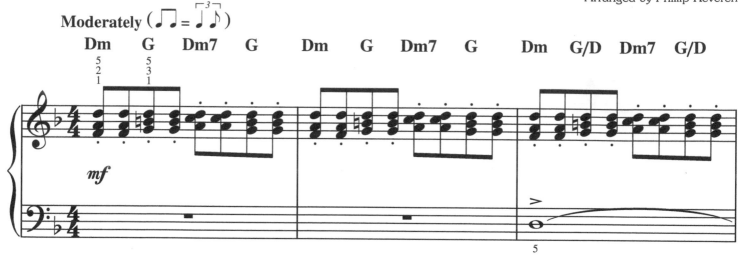

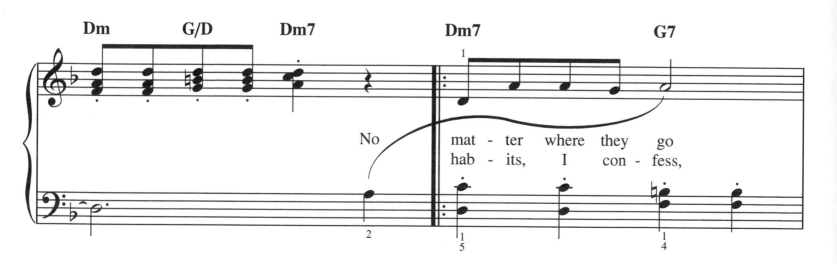

No mat - ter where they go
hab - its, I con - fess,

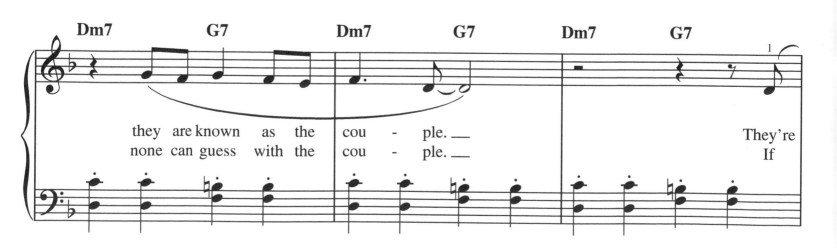

they are known as the cou - ple. ___
none can guess with the cou - ple. ___

They're
If

THEME FROM "STAR TREK®"

from the Paramount Television Series STAR TREK

Words by GENE RODDENBERRY
Music by ALEXANDER COURAGE
Arranged by Phillip Keveren

Slowly, rubato

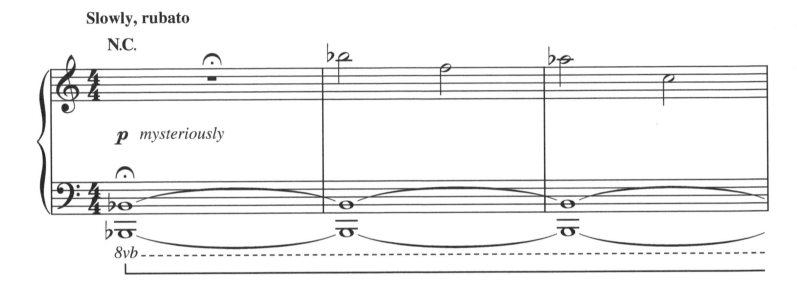

Maestoso

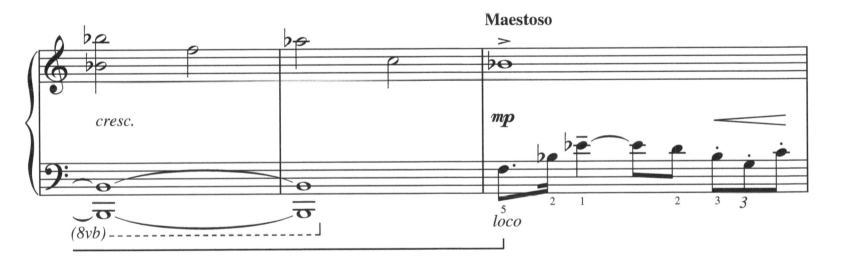

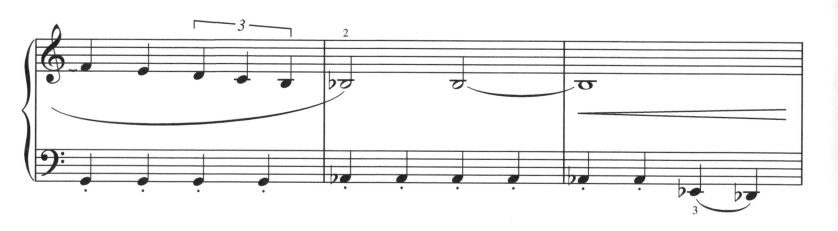

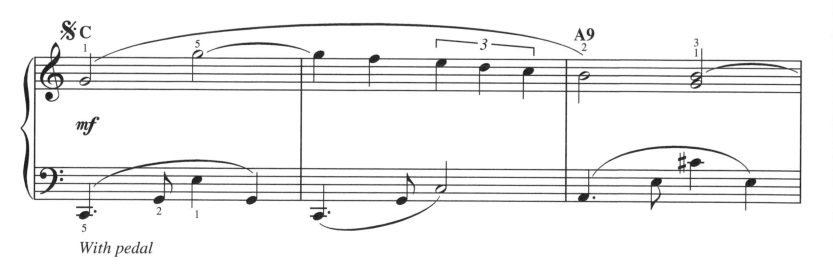

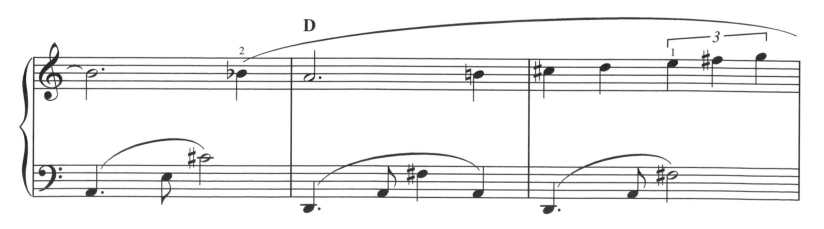

SESAME STREET THEME

Words by BRUCE HART,
JON STONE and JOE RAPOSO
Music by JOE RAPOSO
Arranged by Phillip Keveren

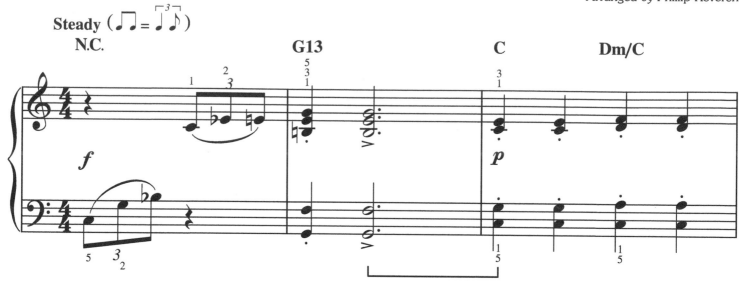

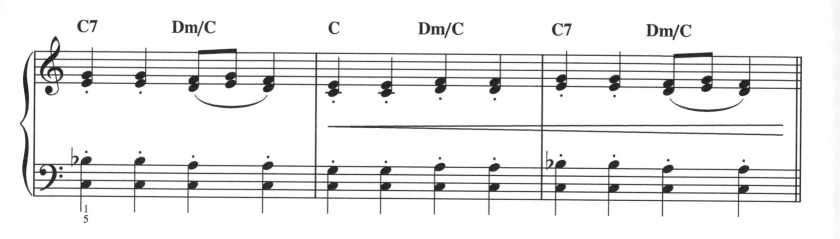

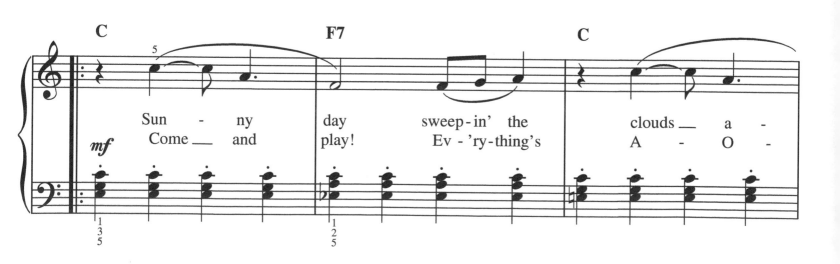

Sun - ny   day   sweep-in' the   clouds __ a -
Come __ and   play!   Ev - 'ry-thing's   A - O -

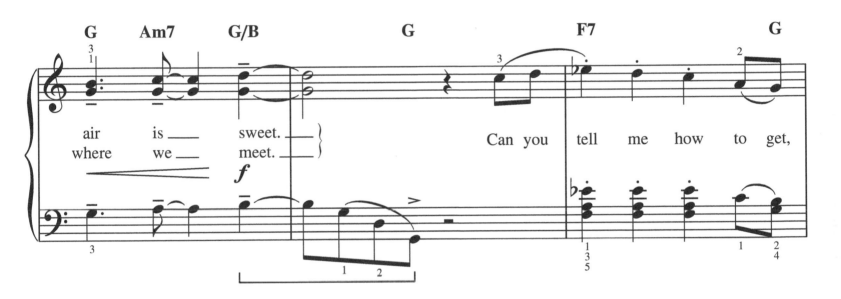

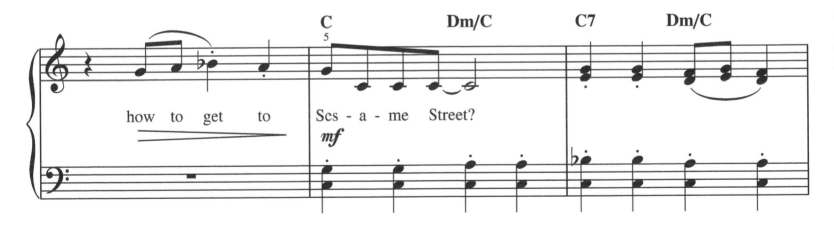

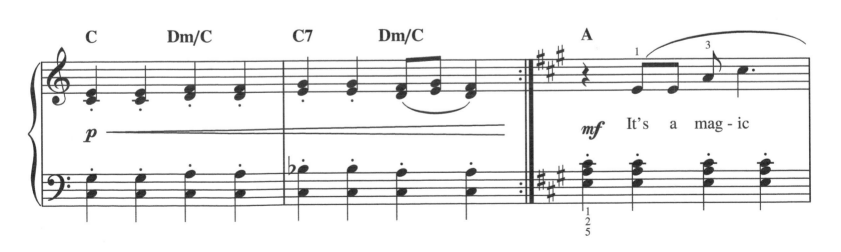

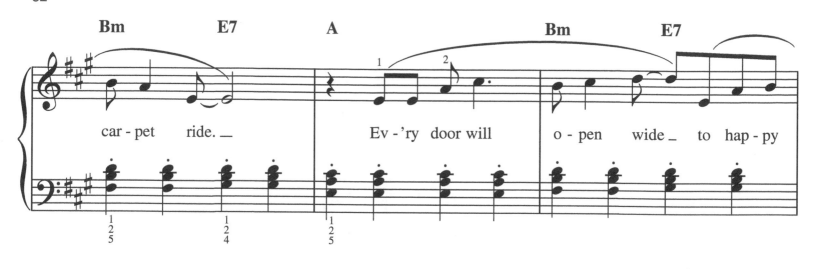

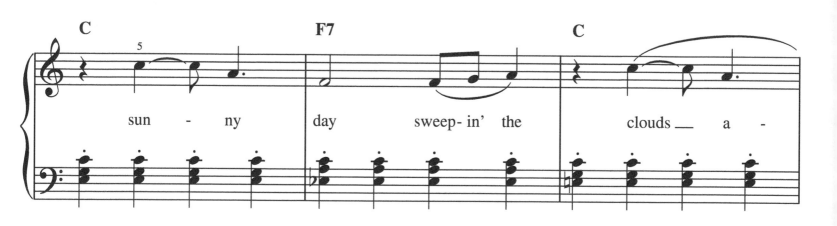

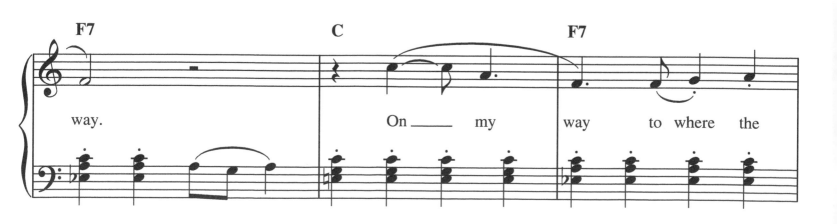

WHERE EVERYBODY KNOWS YOUR NAME

Theme from the Paramount Television Series CHEERS

Words and Music by GARY PORTNOY
and JUDY HART ANGELO
Arranged by Phillip Keveren

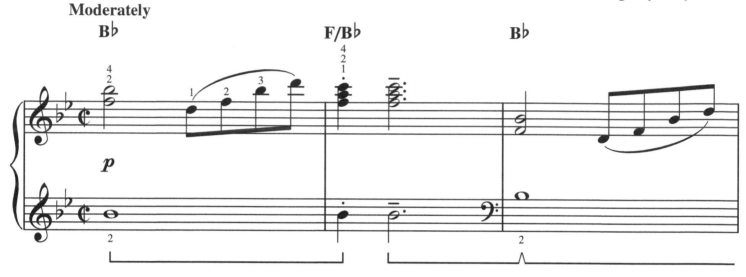

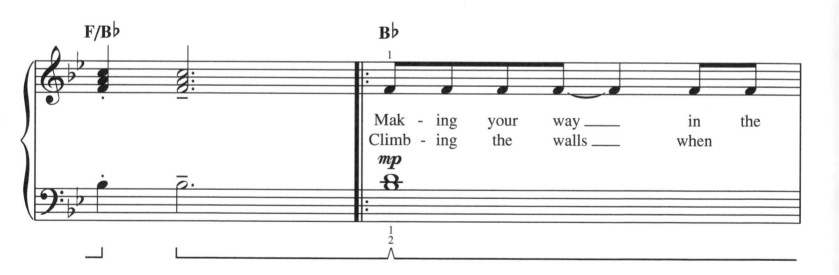

Mak - ing your way in the
Climb - ing the walls when

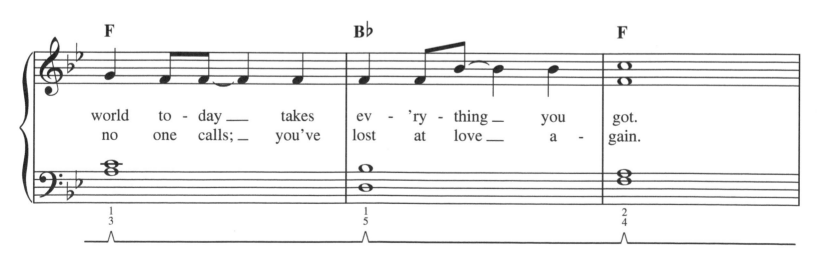

world to - day takes ev - 'ry - thing you got.
no one calls; you've lost at love a - gain.

You wan - na go _____ where

ev - 'ry - bod - y knows

your name.

WINGS
Theme from the Paramount Television Series WINGS

"Sonata In A" by FRANZ SCHUBERT
as Adapted and Arranged by ANTONY COOKE
Arranged by Phillip Keveren

WON'T YOU BE MY NEIGHBOR?
(It's a Beautiful Day in This Neighborhood)
from MISTER ROGERS' NEIGHBORHOOD

Words and Music by
FRED ROGERS
Arranged by Phillip Keveren

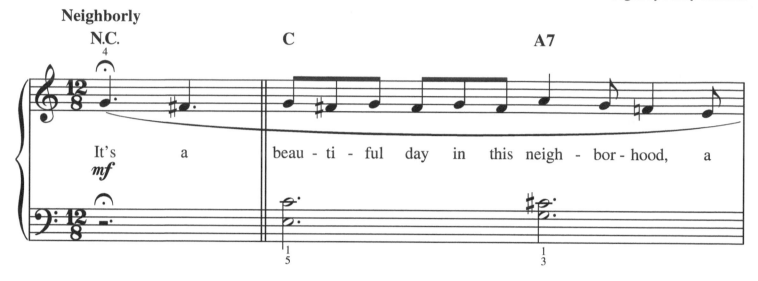

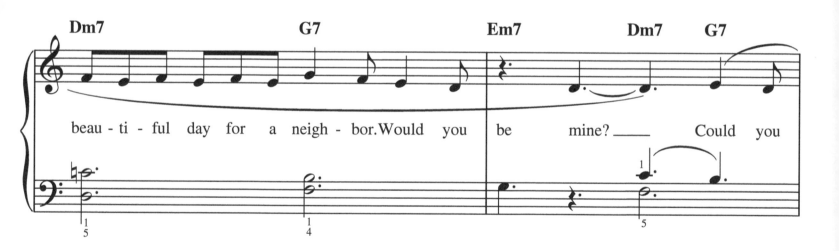

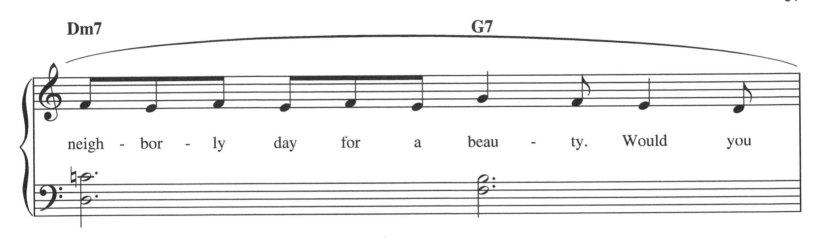

neigh - bor - ly day for a beau - ty. Would you

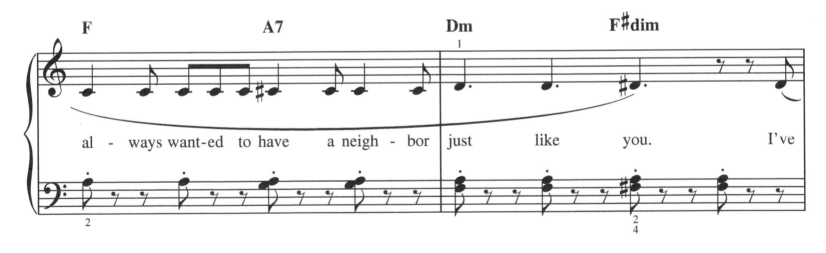

be mine? Could you be mine? I have

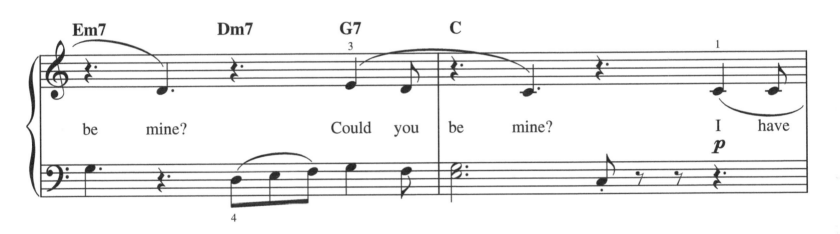

al - ways want-ed to have a neigh - bor just like you. I've

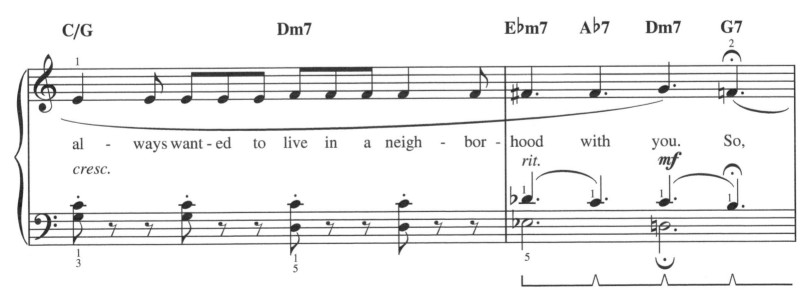

al - ways want-ed to live in a neigh - bor-hood with you. So,

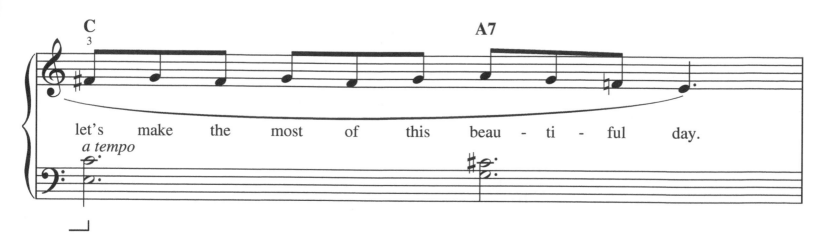

let's make the most of this beau - ti - ful day.
a tempo

Since we're to - geth - er we might as well say, "Would you be mine? Could you be mine?

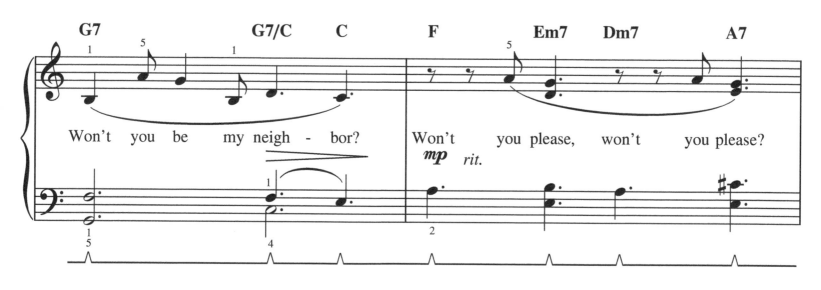

Won't you be my neigh - bor? Won't you please, won't you please?
mp *rit.*

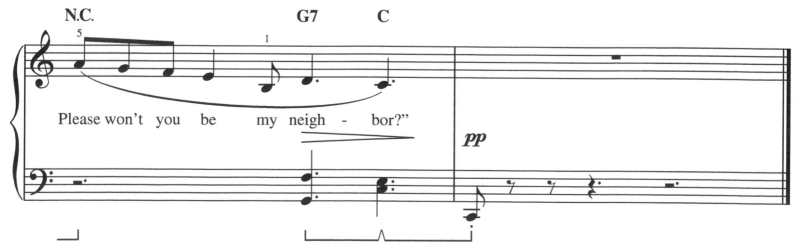

Please won't you be my neigh - bor?"
pp

THE PHILLIP KEVEREN SERIES

PIANO SOLO

ABBA FOR CLASSICAL PIANO
00156644.............................$14.99

ABOVE ALL
00311024.............................$12.99

BACH MEETS JAZZ
00198473.............................$14.99

THE BEATLES
00306412.............................$16.99

THE BEATLES FOR CLASSICAL PIANO
00312189.............................$14.99

THE BEATLES – RECITAL SUITES
00275876.............................$19.99

BEST PIANO SOLOS
00312546.............................$14.99

BLESSINGS
00156601.............................$12.99

BLUES CLASSICS
00198656.............................$12.99

BROADWAY'S BEST
00310669.............................$14.99

A CELTIC CHRISTMAS
00310629.............................$12.99

THE CELTIC COLLECTION
00310549.............................$12.95

CELTIC SONGS WITH A CLASSICAL FLAIR
00280571.............................$12.99

CHRISTMAS MEDLEYS
00311414.............................$12.99

CHRISTMAS AT THE MOVIES
00312190.............................$14.99

CHRISTMAS SONGS FOR CLASSICAL PIANO
00233788.............................$12.99

CINEMA CLASSICS
00310607.............................$14.99

CLASSICAL JAZZ
00311083.............................$12.95

COLDPLAY FOR CLASSICAL PIANO
00137779.............................$15.99

DISNEY RECITAL SUITES
00249097.............................$16.99

DISNEY SONGS FOR CLASSICAL PIANO
00311754.............................$16.99

DISNEY SONGS FOR RAGTIME PIANO
00241379.............................$16.99

THE FILM SCORE COLLECTION
00311811.............................$14.99

FOLKSONGS WITH A CLASSICAL FLAIR
00269408.............................$12.99

GOLDEN SCORES
00233789.............................$14.99

GOSPEL GREATS
00144351.............................$12.99

GREAT STANDARDS
00311157.............................$12.95

THE HYMN COLLECTION
00311071.............................$12.99

HYMN MEDLEYS
00311349.............................$12.99

HYMNS IN A CELTIC STYLE
00280705.............................$12.99

HYMNS WITH A CLASSICAL FLAIR
00269407.............................$12.99

HYMNS WITH A TOUCH OF JAZZ
00311249.............................$12.99

JINGLE JAZZ
00310762.............................$14.99

BILLY JOEL FOR CLASSICAL PIANO
00175310.............................$15.99

ELTON JOHN FOR CLASSICAL PIANO
00126449.............................$15.99

LET FREEDOM RING!
00310839.............................$12.99

ANDREW LLOYD WEBBER
00313227.............................$15.99

MANCINI MAGIC
00313523.............................$14.99

MORE DISNEY SONGS FOR CLASSICAL PIANO
00312113.............................$15.99

MOTOWN HITS
00311295.............................$12.95

PIAZZOLLA TANGOS
00306870.............................$15.99

QUEEN FOR CLASSICAL PIANO
00156645.............................$15.99

RICHARD RODGERS CLASSICS
00310755.............................$15.99

SHOUT TO THE LORD!
00310699.............................$14.99

SONGS FROM CHILDHOOD FOR EASY CLASSICAL PIANO
00233688.............................$12.99

THE SOUND OF MUSIC
00119403.............................$14.99

SYMPHONIC HYMNS FOR PIANO
00224738.............................$14.99

TIN PAN ALLEY
00279673.............................$12.99

TREASURED HYMNS FOR CLASSICAL PIANO
00312112.............................$14.99

THE TWELVE KEYS OF CHRISTMAS
00144926.............................$12.99

YULETIDE JAZZ
00311911.............................$17.99

EASY PIANO

AFRICAN-AMERICAN SPIRITUALS
00310610.............................$10.99

CATCHY SONGS FOR PIANO
00218387.............................$12.99

CELTIC DREAMS
00310973.............................$10.95

CHRISTMAS CAROLS FOR EASY CLASSICAL PIANO
00233686.............................$12.99

CHRISTMAS POPS
00311126.............................$14.99

CLASSIC POP/ROCK HITS
00311548.............................$12.95

A CLASSICAL CHRISTMAS
00310769.............................$10.95

CLASSICAL MOVIE THEMES
00310975.............................$12.99

CONTEMPORARY WORSHIP FAVORITES
00311805.............................$14.99

DISNEY SONGS FOR EASY CLASSICAL PIANO
00144352.............................$12.99

EARLY ROCK 'N' ROLL
00311093.............................$12.99

GEORGE GERSHWIN CLASSICS
00110374.............................$12.99

GOSPEL TREASURES
00310805.............................$12.99

THE VINCE GUARALDI COLLECTION
00306821.............................$16.99

HYMNS FOR EASY CLASSICAL PIANO
00160294.............................$12.99

IMMORTAL HYMNS
00310798.............................$12.99

JAZZ STANDARDS
00311294.............................$12.99

LOVE SONGS
00310744.............................$12.99

THE MOST BEAUTIFUL SONGS FOR EASY CLASSICAL PIANO
00233740.............................$12.99

POP STANDARDS FOR EASY CLASSICAL PIANO
00233739.............................$12.99

RAGTIME CLASSICS
00311293.............................$10.95

SONGS FROM CHILDHOOD FOR EASY CLASSICAL PIANO
00233688.............................$12.99

SONGS OF INSPIRATION
00103258.............................$12.99

TIMELESS PRAISE
00310712.............................$12.95

10,000 REASONS
00126450.............................$14.99

TV THEMES
00311086.............................$12.99

21 GREAT CLASSICS
00310717.............................$12.99

WEEKLY WORSHIP
00145342.............................$16.99

BIG-NOTE PIANO

CHILDREN'S FAVORITE MOVIE SONGS
00310838.............................$12.99

CHRISTMAS MUSIC
00311247.............................$10.95

CLASSICAL FAVORITES
00277368.............................$12.99

CONTEMPORARY HITS
00310907.............................$12.99

DISNEY FAVORITES
00277370.............................$14.99

JOY TO THE WORLD
00310888.............................$10.95

THE NUTCRACKER
00310908.............................$10.99

STAR WARS
00277371.............................$16.99

BEGINNING PIANO SOLOS

AWESOME GOD
00311202.............................$12.99

CHRISTIAN CHILDREN'S FAVORITES
00310837.............................$12.99

CHRISTMAS FAVORITES
00311246.............................$10.95

CHRISTMAS TIME IS HERE
00311334.............................$12.99

CHRISTMAS TRADITIONS
00311117.............................$10.99

EASY HYMNS
00311250.............................$12.99

EVERLASTING GOD
00102710.............................$10.99

JAZZY TUNES
00311403.............................$10.95

PIANO DUET

CLASSICAL THEME DUETS
00311350.............................$10.99

HYMN DUETS
00311544.............................$12.99

PRAISE & WORSHIP DUETS
00311203.............................$12.99

STAR WARS
00119405.............................$14.99

WORSHIP SONGS FOR TWO
00253545.............................$12.99

HAL•LEONARD®

Visit **www.halleonard.com**
for a complete series listing.

Prices, contents, and availability subject to change without notice.